Beyond the Sea
ANNE FITZGERALD

salmonpoetry

Published in 2012 by
Salmon Poetry
Cliffs of Moher, County Clare, Ireland
Website: www.salmonpoetry.com
Email: info@salmonpoetry.com

ISBN 978-1-908836-20-5

COVER ARTWORK:
Dublin Bay with Cloud Sky (2002), reproduced by kind permission of the artist, George Potter RHA. Photography by Gillian Buckley, courtesy of Taylor Galleries.
AUTHOR PHOTOGRAPH: © Therese Aherne
COVER DESIGN & TYPESETTING: *Siobhán Hutson*

Salmon Poetry receives financial support from The Arts Council

For Michael and Thomas.
And to Aileen Gaughran-Khatib.

Acknowledgements

are due to the editors of the following publications in which some of these poems or earlier versions of them first appeared:

E.ratio, Freeverse, The Irish Catullus, The Moth, New Hibernian Review, Plains Song Review, Prairie Schooner, The Recorder, Stand Magazine, Stonecutter, The Watchful Heart: A New Generation of Poets and *The Windsor Review.*

I wish to thank Andrew Carpenter, Frank McGuinness, Thornfield Poets and Jonathon Williams, and at Salmon: Siobhán Hutson and Jessie Lendennie.

I should like to thank Michael Ondaatje and his publishers, McClelland & Stewart, Random House, and Bloomsbury for permission to quote from *Divisadero*.

In addition, I am most grateful to Kieran McLaughlin and The Ireland Fund of Monaco for a residential bursary in 2007 and to Géraldine Lance of The Princess Grace Irish Library, Monaco.

There is a hidden presence of others in us, even those we have known briefly. We contain them for the rest of our lives, at every border that we cross.

—MICHAEL ONDAATJE,
Divisadero

Contents

Dévotion

It makes sense all the same when you think of it. Born
on the feast of finding the true cross, he'd always felt
a direct line, so to speak. Since Johnny gave up the drink
he's killed worrying them blasted rosary beads to death,
his prints will surely be left on some glorious mystery
like a pilgrim crossing the Mayflower's gangway, ready
to set sail. Just like the sail Johnny hoists through the neck
of a Jameson twelve year old. Launches it of a Friday
in the Black Swan's back bar, where Nelly Regan's pink
paddling pool might well be the lake in Central Park.
For miles they does come to re-enact crusades, to seek
indulgences for battles lost, run ripples in full sail, sack
purveyors of high castle walls, pray turret slits a melody
of martyrs, tall flags wave colour askew as if a tapestry
lost in a watered-down detail of its own threaded myth.

Diminished Responsibility

On shank's mare he made his way across the terrain, with not a sinner in sight to a place beyond where Loopline porter is not usually drunk. Aye, not a dickey -pricky-bird is heard about himself and him out picking fluffy buttercups to beat

the band of late, his birdie gauge of sorts. He'd head round the town after dark chin-seeking young ones to yellow his eve 'n the likes, and she giving him what for *the Dallaho, whack for the Dally ho*...Holy Thursday's feet washing night alright, though none can whole heartily confess to know what happened actually. Yet it diminishes not what passed off like odd loyalty on the bridge of discovery.

Post Mortem

As the pathologist declares
a number of body parts missing,
on further examination it proves

John Doe's stray hairs will be found
strewn about Mary Hathaway's hair lip
after his lips did cushions her sweet little-bits
like a slug on the back of a veined dogleaf.

Imagine, eggnog stains his cupid's bow
like a soft yolk doffing a cap at a mustard seed.
Pleads he do, with Lucy-Leachy Brennan to command
a royal performance not seen for a month of Sundays.

His hands Trudy Wilcox from over the ways hips
claimed, and as for the eyes, went astray they say
looking for happiness in peculiar little hot spots,

from the ridges of the Appalachians to silica under
foot at Reykjavík's geothermal spa, where Mary-Joe Kenny
from Slivenamon resembles the pale moon rising

out of marshmallow whiteness at the Blue Lagoon,
as a loon's wing beat is breaking silence over a Killarney
lake, a camera clicks as if a neck snap from every

which angle, shows his soul still intact, unsullied by
this rush of blood to John Doe's delicate little head.
His medulla oblongata resembles violets found on bog oak.

Ryan Lacken of Lackabeg

Early on talk was he is off his trolley, what with him out
hammering heavy rain and all, in a rig-out fit for a duck,
them Russian ones that Baltic tail-winds doest west-propel
across the Atlantic to Booterstown, emerald breasted ripple-winds.
When not charm'n birds from trees or bringing virgins up to speed
he had that great honest touch of a tealeaf about him, so he did,
light-fingering his conquests as if the Norman one, whispering sweet
-nothings or sweet f-all, if the truth be known. For d'most part
they'd slip oak 'n ash under his lead, plant a peck on his sunny south
whilst he did dip in and out of all in sundry to beat the band
...*on the run*... no less, disseminating his little red ridings over
his make-believe Sherwood, when not up-ending a bottle of its finest
over his curried chips of a Saturday after he lays upon his willow
goes to Bo-Peep; in such sleep, peep-shows run ninety to the dozen.

Circuitry

A touch discommoded, none d'less your
rig-out is a modest enough attempt to
placate your former profession. Though,
days are when I can't but help wonder,
might you not be more your good self
in a wet suit and goggles, a wind 'n surf
display, splayed for all the world to see.
A Biggles at the head of our stair, as you
duck 'n dive d'onslaught of imaginary
B52's. In the end, sunlight skewers you,
just like stain glass on the return, gives
way as though a brain scan detecting colour
defects, illuminates darkness in prefrontal
lobes as if manuscripts of old, or a riot
of neon down Broadway, works its
way into the scent of memory banks.

Sweet Nothings

All morning clouds have being gathering, cold fronts
collide to produce a depression coming from the east,
as pineapple winds makes free with the Canadian
coastline. Goose Village disappears into the annals.
Channels it does, the manner in which the true history
of d'fruit machine will be regaled, as will the size of
nickels 'n dimes, decimalisation and fluctuating currency
rates, blind dates 'n ancient saints, creates interest in
troubled states of soulless mates: Huntley 'n Carr, nay
mention Judas or Pilot, apostolic treasures purpling
ecclesial secret ring kissers. Blisters, Mrs Elders gets
from Dick Devine's little ceremonies of love, like cobras
on the hot Sahara floor, snakes time out in grains,
ridges in the aftermath for sandologists to measure pleasure.

Longing

From the sound of things you say
he's as hard as that stick of rock

young Jim Long's Jack brought
back last May twelve months, to suck

as leaves fall crisp, and Jenny scores
ochre skin, cuts two eyes 'n a mouth out,

lobotomises soft pink tissue, fingers
pith 'n seeds, takes insides out,

blind-bakes pastry for pumpkin pie
before she sews brown buttons for Guy's

eyes, effigy of her own little gun powder
plot, plit-plotting away with the fairies,

whilst twee-twee flappers circle as if twists
of chalk askew, like aunt Lily's wild

vermilion lippy, she'll smear along
Jack's long back; tracing his discs,

as a castaway in search of an island,
her lip-hush kisses sail his vertebrae

like her index over the spine of an upturned
hull beached in the scent of bladderwrack.

In the Oral Tradition

Throw us over a package of them, what's it thingies,
don't you know the yokes, them what's it again?
Yea, those *Manhattan dry roasted*. Them's the lads.
Good for mouth-cupping, though d'dry roast can catch
the throat as if to choke. On more occasions than one
I did think I was a gonner. Imagine coroner's report,
...death by misadventures nut, caught in gullet...,
shocking way to go. Though, wasn't it Jack Stacks
cousin once removed, swallowed a pheasant pellet
shot. Shot to hell he was, in that rare bit of game.
Blame was apportioned in part, to his Thai child
bride. Her neck they say, craned like a turkey cock,
over his open mouth, to make sure her round lump
of little lead had lodged in his oversized larynx, just so.

Quack-Doctoring

In the event of a nuclear accident potassium tablets is yer only man.
Remember, arm yourself: knitted gloves, scarf and hat will do the trick
like gold-shot with green when sunlight hits an afternoon Martini, vodka
gin lined, olive brimmed, salt figures equations out, out of nowhere,
as if dust breath-blown into air. For movement California Syrup of Figs try,
and for chesty troubles rub Camphorate Oil into affected parts thoroughly
then there's poor man's plaster not to mention d'avocado Epson Salts tin,
d'red of Zubes and spearmint-blue of Vicks, rubs deep seated coughs away
with the birdies, as if skies cleared by gunshot. Nothing. Then silence turns
a rustle of grass, a blade whistled between thumbs, a gamekeeper's gamey
eye thumbs 'n fingers his trigger happy long barrel, cocked for the ready
as a mallard webs it to water, past reeds and the one, young poacher Jack
breaths through, keeps mum, recalls weaving St. Bridget's crosses as duck
á la orange bears its own pellet cross ... *give us our daily trespasses...*'er's.

Watching Weather

You are a trifle put out to say the least, not to mention lessened by the whole
experience to say the least, to take you in hand, not wait hand 'n foot, would
be the thing, thing is…*are you right there Michael, are you right…*you're away
with d'birdies at Days Inn, glued to Stan, Rita and Katrina too. Kat breaks city
barrier walls, waters drown homes; your leaning tower of Pisa brought back
floats as if a steamship funnel knocked on its side, Archimedes principles apply
not. Bush's Connie shops on Fifth for fancy shoes, whilst a black Labrador dead
to the world keeps Mrs Lynch company, spills the beans crossing the river Styx,
neighbours cloudless livelihoods… *do you think you'll be home before the night…*
As if autumnal leaves, fallen pages of Gideon's Bible meet their maker, religiosity
watertight no more, blots; blessed believe and the will of God right out of sight
like potato blight, grassed mouths green already dead-beat on made-up road names
naming strangers, points our home place out, arcs dome-like the New Orleans
one. Oh, dear ocean pearly-whirly-girly…*Michael row your boat ashore, Alleluia…*

Tuscany

No kids ride yellow burnt sienna horses, piazzas holds weather at bay,
stillness fills cumulus clouds with the ease of rain falling up lands
in elsewhere arches where wisteria threads Corinthian pillars, masks
stone faces, trace its grain as the pupil dilates, diminishes to a pin-prick
in Florence without a Pope like the shadow aspect of faded frescos,
knowledge colours its application of, jade-ochre, pigments skin-pink,
as flat rose tinted windows catch earlier shadow-light of a faded dusk
whilst sun skewers the features of saints, puts colour in their faces back
to back, illuminates fractures and bruises to the index, got pealing apples
in tart making pursuit, pastry rolled and egg washed for hundred 'n eighty
degrees as the albumin congeals: flour self-raises, heat holds air airborne,
so it does, binds wheat bathed under a harvest moon, wide off the mark
like a prince that has abdicated or an ecclesial heresy, a cutting away.

Light in the Darkness

Between two and five they comes, mostly
of their own will, though willed on a bit
a' times too. First comes Curl Brien, only
sees faces, never rabbits in new moons,
turns over and over her thru'penny bit,
finger–held since Independence, falls
flat on its monarch's head on each full
phase, as she be swat'n them–there blue
bottles till the cows come home, home.
Curl Brien would swat flies till cows come
home, or her Johnnie's key darkens its lock
in d'absence of light. From nowhere, a wick
between his fasting spit 'n movements offside
receives the full fuzzy pleasures of its dew.

The Joy of Mixology

With her palms moulded firmly around Sunlight
Chambers' finest carbolic, she fingers and thumbs
a lather into existence, sees the death of roundness
circle itself as if a fossil forming structures of shape.
Not unlike the ones she threw that night in Dick Love's
snug, back in seventy-three. By closing time her fetish
for Singapore Slings has diminished to a whim for Rob
-Roys, Sex on the Beach and for mint leaves lightly
bruised by white Havana Club, Mojitos be the dozen
score no identifiable mark on her altered sensibility.
Mondays are Manhattans. Tuesday and Wednesdays
seem to slip into Long Island Iced Teas, quite naturally.
By mid week dullness pours itself into all and sundry,
taints as Vermeer's varnish might, an Old Fashioned.
Sundays are spent in prayer, she communes with purity
in Gibson's: dry vermouth with pearl cocktail onions.

Caché

Word got out, he peers
 into the back of railway

clocks between two and four.
Counts his stacks of butter

as though national reserves,
fingering greaseproof nuggets

releases a kind of pleasure
not realised, turns half-pounds

as if sovereigns in decline, marks
the true hue his yellow gold leaf

between tic 'n tock of a hair's
breadth, imagines oyster movements

shucking little shells for pearls
of wisdom to yield knowledge

aplenty like an unreliable narrator
bringing things home to roost

at cock-crow, as though hollyhocks
scattered by an abandoned railway.

Pigments and Hues

Partridges you sends, on receipt of my candied
pears, procured from pantry's deep darkness
where low slung light swings late summer fruits
to d'fore, illuminates green seeds in raspberry
jam, preserves lined 'n labelled, dates look back
in your copperplate hand, that drupelets burst in,
not unlike walls of d'fresco-boyos, Fra, n' Giotto.
Whose banquets draw guests into flat candlelight,
till perspective finds roundness. Lady's smock
cardamine and borage, borders tablecloths aplenty,
with tiny bouquets of lovage, savory and tansy.
An orange tip butterfly feasts upon brittleness,
outlines movement's frailty of ultramarine phases
shadowing Naples yellow's in pools of red lakes.

Passion

In the heel of d'hunt it matters not
a jot that your leathery sling, shot

through many a fractured thought
whole and hearty, or that you ought

consider other cheaper ideas bought
to curry favour and the like, sought

after hand over fist. Fact is Dirk Fisk
lulls you Minnie Stoppard, for a tryst

down Lockhart Lane, past fish 'n chip
shops, where Molly Charley does back

street botch-jobs, beside the man who
raises red sails on Galway Hookers

inside the glass domes of bottles. Lets
you discover Dirk's true tender nature,

uncovers his rabbit hole ease, purely
to appease the day he'll wave a sawn

-off about a pool of secretaries, as if bees
making for eaves, as the clickety-click-clack

of shorthand-typists type long ranging keys
to the rhythm of cartridge reloads, before soft

landings are found in your left hemisphere,
as a breeze flurries knees, knee deep in crimson.

For the Love of Things

Was Ascension Thursday, so by its very nature,
no wonder he brought things to a new level

of consciousness, talking of his mother
of pearl inlayed card table, brought back from Brazil

in seventy-two, a keepsake to turn a trick
on, or simply to stroke, along with his Jane Russell

look-alike who exchange nuptials after two whole
weeks, and will prove a handful for his grasp,

despite his light fingered touch. A good head
on her shoulders is what's said. Though, if truth

be told it be the keenness of her eye draws most
towards her, some says it be the ochre fleck

encroaching her pupil, does it every time, as if a fly
caught in resin, swimming the sticky limits of amber,

colours his emotions and ability to achieve full
houses or straight runs of sweet little flushes.

After Catullus IX

Veranius, the apple of my eye by three-hundred arms-length,
out of all my buddies,
have you come back then, home and dry
to your loving brothers and elderly mother?
Yes you have; tickled-pink with the news I am.
I shall see your safe return, listen to you
telling tales of the nation's past, and its diverse tribes of Hibernians,
as you do, and luring your neck next to mine
I shall kiss your smitten mouth and eyes.
Oh, of all fair-haired men holier,
is none more satisfied and sanctified than I?

Pen Pal

From Calcutta you sends seeds,
stuck between onion skin
aerogram leaves 'n copperplate
curves of black Indian ink
sealed with your fasting spit,
that's held its tongue across:
the Himalayas, Kashmir,
and the Caspian, till I peel it back
all fingers 'n thumbs; it spills
as if d'Ganges' mouth into my lap.

Pure Fiction

to Shane Harrison

The year d'flying duck flew off the wall of flock, Eva peals paper layers right back,
to Clarice Cliff reds and Monet yellows, douse and dabs warm water to its brow
as if fever suffering, soak to peel stubborn glue from plaster even hack mortar off in
d'offing, reveals Joe Stanley's waxy green, One Nine One Seven, rayon-crayon writ,
borders his Morris floral run, runs carmine, as if a John Waterhouse sketch-study in
profile. Stylistically he's a touch of d'pre-Raph about him, dapper 'n swish, open neck
'n curls in flight-spirals, his Adam's Apple sports to all in sundry as if a firm ripe Cox
ready for some young maiden's pearly whites. Sips, Eva does, her Jack D on d'rocks,
as if a Tio Pepe, releases a pale imitation not oak matured, afraid she is to knock back
for fear of a liking this palomino grape, a dry pretender of Italian not Kentucky sun.

Done to death that auld horse chestnut Rea Looney trots about as if Carrickmacross
lace, laid out like a bare faced lie or a Wedgwood ring holder, along d'runner running
like gossip, open secrets insinuates themselves into the lives of others, in songbird
hours, echoes staccatos as if rain-quavers galvanised darkness' deep sweet crevices
of tempo-rubato before the silence of d'first note contracts, releases unwritten sonatas.
If it's not one thing it's another, what with you on your high-bloody-hobby horse, rock
rocking like a bin or a sin on a slow release in the garden of moral polemic delights,
light lighting as if a Christmas tree at sea. See. A tanker stills a cargo of non nationals.
Trafficking completes some hierarchy of need that bleeds a national epidemic of greed,
feeds culture to a seedless breath like cant-creeds, incanting the coolness of mosques,

sways air 'n Joe-Jack's way of seeing for his vision's set on some foreign mystic's sun
or version thereof, that sends devoted backpackers into crowds, reporters accounts of
debris round tree stumps and d'national front tow party lines as if playing blind man's
bluff…toot-toot pouts from Mr. 'n Mrs. so and so from up and down d'road, stood on
sidelines as Joe-Jack's Civil Service promotion is sidelined for Ballinasloe Barbie's
hourglass shadow-knowledge of figures, not to mention her fingering of figurines.
Pinkeen's Sally Lawler picks away at, at the back of the 7A, going up Glenageary Hill
heading towards d'Noggin with a naggin of Paddy Power. Its gold label; a holy medal
faces heaven from a Tesco hold-all, glints it does in sunlight as though Keats' bright star.
Are you sure? Yes, and that bar, snug beside Auto-Tyre and Jehovah's Witness Hall

has pheasants hung over Guinness pumps, as drinkers swallow feathers 'n shot, a sell
out no less for a taste of d'hunting season. Reason has it for some or other, Nora Jolly
skipped town as fluently as Cinnamon Boyd's words under thumb, in his Peter 'n Jane
reader for grown ups. Ups-a-daisy, there she goes, young Philomena McGillacuddy off

on the pull again. Lloyd Grossman's Corma sauce patterns her Laura Ashley paisley
shirt, as Ian says, *No Never*. Then a Molly Bloom, *Yes-Yes-Yes*, for red handed Ulster.
Yes to the British, opens trade and the Stock Exchange to McGuinness and Paisley,
the NYSE gavel comes down. Bell rings. Trading begins hosted by the Ireland Funds.
Asunder is what Sally Lawler is, all a; in that pheasant hung bar knocking back shots
of holy water as though at Knock shrine, at a loss for prayer as Joe-Jack saunters by

lone-rangerly without a gigi to his name. Tame for a few scoops, then goes on the lash
like the kingfisher on the Kiskadee label, dips his orange beak a little too liberally.
Bash and crash, down comes ashtray: butts freefall as if parachutes opening in a mist
of ash after Pompeii. *Stay, why don't you for another*, Joe-Jack presses, young Sally.
O'Brien, is it? and the way she might look at you…on that old Harp ad, sun-kissed in
days of open windowed Ford Cortina prophesies, from handheld speakers; Haughey's
vision for a New Ireland, spreads with gusto d'length and breath of hedgerow like rain
falling on deaf ears. Il Duce-like as he sails from the Mirabeau to his own Byzantium,
Inishvickillane. And as droves leave from: Bray to Baltimore, Newport to Newhaven,
Dalkey to Dartmouth, from the mouths of canals and riverbeds they do come, to bed

down in towns that sells goldfish with packets of King crisps, pickled eggs or bacon
fries with every half dozen large stout. Ticket touts shout the odds. *Anyone buying or
selling, buying or selling*, outside Wrigley Field's, Radio City and off-off Broadway,
in alleyways by The Olympia and The Gaiety Theatres where players strut their stuff.
Tough as nails is what Joe-Jack reckons Sally Lawler is, not receptive to me charms.
Couldn't be the full shilling and her fiddling about with auld Pat Bailey's firm Coxes.
Unseemly it is, and her up there like a church mouse reading Revelations of a Sunday
then bandies Psalms about in Gimlet hazes, seeking the perfect mix Sally says, half
gin half *Roses Lime*, the length 'n breadth of the 7A bar-stool-route. Routed to d'spot
some say. Others no danger she'll get scurvy or have to walk the plank. Lanky Hank

Ryan Williams gives his namesake a spin on the jukebox's turntable. *Honky Tonkin*
spills as if mixers into drinks, 'n I saw the Light, catches dank tumbler bottoms heaven
bound. Bound into night, heading for hills who seeks valleys a–plenty as if creamery
managers at Potín stills for ill gotten gain after dark, puts a kick into milky churns.
Turns out, Sally Lawler's had a step or two out with Edward Brick Lyons of d'Rocks,
beyond Cary's middle meadow where horse chestnuts crack open over night fires.
Burns bright as a harvest moon or Joyce Blaney's pocket-turning sovereign, picked
from her Ma's coat hem, who'd plucked it off Fr. Dan's fake parish mahogany plate.
Be great if it pays Joyce's fare across the Channel. Word on the street; *Blaney's fond
of her drop*. Her liver gives up d'ghost and Fr. Dan's son, on the outskirts of Essex.

T-Rex blares from Thatcher's kingdom, adjacent to church halls 'n Women Institutes, bolstering Rock of Ages 'n Victoria sponge buns, butterfly-winged in search of flight, prayer wheels and books, altar-boys' open palms holds the lace weight of religiosity. Incense burns. Prayerful smoke trails darkness, fades into congregations as if victims. Slim-Jims full to the brim with Beefeater's, languish in knobs of ice as if a see-through gin palace on counter tops. Watch and chain hang upside down from young Sally Lawler's left breast, stopped at three, remnant of spoils from her Bethnal Green days. Shifts Florence might have shy'd from. Her pioneer pin's lost to cable 'n blackberry. Fables abound about her night duty, on Sealink Ferry crossings from here to there. Bear in mind her's is lost to finding her own true love, Paddy Power. Hours they does

spend, remembering to forget. Threats of rain are imminent as Joe-Jack hovers like a thunder cloud ready to burst. First to fill Sally's glass, later offers a Morris Minor spin be moonlight. From dizzy heights, escapades and city lights they does see. Sees darkness illuminate home fires burn as truths, soothsayers layer myth as if a build up of wallpaper. Papers cracks, misadventures 'n diminished responsibility, easy as you like. Flight is imminent with them blasted flying ducks again. On the train home, just past the bird sanctuary Sally peers into light shafts making for some bloke's fly reading the FT no less, makes its way beneath his Crombie. Recalls she do, how opening teeth of farm machinery receive harvests, and of slow pulling purple-white turnips from warm earth, runs her hand

ever so, along trunks, feels groves to the root, holds the ebb n' flow of shape itself. From a walled garden near Cricklewood, Eva's pallet develops a taste for Bombay Gin before cocktail hour, that angelica, juniper berries and those seeds of paradise does it every time, before Sally carry's hemlock over their threshold where Joe-Jack has no hold. Out of her hold-all; turnips galore, a tin of menthol snuff, 'n Vera Lynn's White Cliffs, plays many a stylus to its death, of hale and hearty fellows well met. Frets Eva does, over what others may say of Sally and her, hanging burgundy flock together, forever. Severs tradition, its mill-run of impossible suns under easy algebraic equations, edging for higher ground, where drowned thoughts will pass waterproof tests, waving off the first faint signs of burst clouds and rainbow arcs.

Inheritance

Because you have the run of the house,
the lay of the land lies open —
in your palm as if an unwrapped gift.

Beyond the Sea

You dream of Zanzibar, of coconuts heat-split, undulating blueness horizon-creased
hulls colonised by barnacles like cardinal points on a map shadows clownfish in

deep pink coral reefs, chair-o'planes sky flying and of hands softened by lanolin
as if something not previously imagined like Salt of Sargasso good for scurvy,

or explorers before Lewis 'n Clark, of Manor houses left after war for asylums
behind a plantation of Scots pine fenced off, before piers walked into oceans,

Defoe's Crusoe or Jacques Cousteau brings flying fish into living rooms, room
was made on your red settee for ocean-going steamers, palm houses and linden

blossom, beyond white poplars and willows billowing as if interrupting a yawn
after a fashion. Whatever happened to the umbrage you took, Lindbergh's baby,

to Houdini's last breath or Custer's Last, as you stand yourself a few swifts from
the Old Stand nightly, whilst watching pink noise snow blizzard television's screen

screening nothing but a plan of inaction, new starts and one for the road, roads
leading to *Glenamaddy* and such like, of God forbids and heavens above, below

a battery of searchlights signals an overture's arrival like Jesus on Palm Sunday,
where handed out green branches are tucked behind pictures, mirrors and holy

water fonts; pines wither, falls to ground till faith is reaffirmed with a new branch
o' the family playing happy families on feast and holy days of bloody obligation.

To clear the decks you'll have to bide your time, not make waves and keep hard
shoulders in sight, like stark rank and file solutions to free-flow imagined futures.

Secrets hide in the lining of your skin, geometry of a life you might have had.
Sky holds its bladder till thunder builds like a Bolshevik on the eve of revolution.

Airmails

Did you hear the latest, all the rage apparently,
this pyramid selling lark, grows like dandelions.

Aunt Hanna's great granddaughter sent some twenty
dollar bills from Illinois no less, sporting a brick family

of pyramids, with visionary Masonic eyes, and an army
of George Washington's, *to keep us honest*, her copper

plated words says: *not for bets or booze, so here's a soft
pack of them Lucky Strikes*, wrapped in a Good Shepherd

novena, *to be read thrice daily* for seven whole sunsets.
Lets indulgences sought hover as if them same-said low

slung clouds that loom, as bamboo shoots are stripped
clean by Pandas in Dublin's a-Zoological Gardens. Droves

head for d'Hudson; or dream of rivers roaming different lands,
say like the Nile flowing into Edfu, Kom Ombo and the Aswan,

paralleling the Red Sea, up above Luxor towards Hurghada
with Suez in sight. Where the Mediterranean flows into d'basins

of Bitter Lakes, opens sea route between Europe and Asia
Minor, Minor, echoes of history pages: Sultans 'n sultanas,

golden turmeric 'n cayenne, rough silken Ottomans colour
the Sinai as if a caravan of rainbows arcing desert sands.

All mounds form little triangles, angling as aspiring pyramids
mirror the divinity of ancient Egyptians and distant cousins.

Garden Route

You know the day I had your ear, Ocean-brim poured forth,
oozed the length and breath of your fasting-spit, spitting-fast
as if filling the cracks of a wall or a story yet to be written.
Look, those are the clouds of Africa, in Grattan's Dublin.
I saw them once, at the corner of Baggot and Fitzwilliam Streets,
filling perspective right up to the edges, cauliflower clouds.

On a day that is dying to be young over the coast of Mossel Bay
hanger doors slide back. An air-fix model I'd glued at six
nuzzles the blind clarity of light, alighting a dirt track runway.
You lie flat on a seat-less one-seater plane, as if inside the body
of a wind-up bird, beside a man who pushes you from a height;
hook up for a tandem parachute jump as though fucking a stranger.
He releases you, into a blue-world freefalling, white-touch,
crash cloud formations, see land design as if an Ordinance Survey.

Cloud-swimming you hold at bay Clifton and Bantry, flat to touch.
Purple roofed squares, black cockroach-cars fly as the crow,
waves crash rock-peaks, sounds like a fly behind net curtains
bellying shape as if jellyfish below my parachute head. Wind
winds itself on the... *road to God knows where...*sailors left letters
in the Post Office Tree, picked up by the next ship heading home.

At Frog Rock we swam under the eye of Dias Cross.
Dragged by breakers. Unable to get beyond circles circling.
Drags us head first bash 'n crashing, a tsunami of sorts, spins
as though in the claw of bulldozer, like the one digging earth
out at the Mellon township, Hout Bay, where Irish build
homes to last, in shanty towns on corrugated hilltops.

And what pray tell did you bring from South Africa?
I brought Venus and Mars, luminescent shaped shells,
pink-oyster purples from a beach with nothing but Ocean.

House-high waves thunder the shore: lightening trumpet
-drums, percussion comes into play. Ahead, wave-highways head
south for Antarctica. Somewhere over Northern Algiers
the KLM airhostess falls short of the truth, with the face
of a disappointed Madonna, tells how as if would-be-saints
Dutch and English, sprung colonies up, spreads like ink
over blotting paper, absorbs blood 'n guts, clouds Table Mountain.

From a school hall a gospel choir sings through a rainstorm.
Listen. Perfect pitch. Hear the soul of a nation rise up to meet
itself, like the harmony of colour unified. Rain rains down gutters,
and shores, shoring up all they have put store in, like pressed flowers
seen through glass. And when we get there what will we do, when we do
that, what's next, after that, what then sang *Plato's Ghost, what then.*

Little Death

Slowly it came, in sun rising
to kiss dawn as

magnolias, fists of winter,
open blossoms pink.

Or is it more the first taste of figs
brings flesh to the fore?

The tip of your tongue teases
unknown pleasures,

releases a kind of jazz
oozing with the after taste

of movement, like little fish
licking the wild Sargasso.

Storm over Manhattan

Couples are making for St. Mark's for cover,
as you cover me with your Donegal tweed
jacket, passed down from your second cousin
once removed, who was removed to Great Ormond
Street after Omagh. Omaha Nebraska you said
worth a trip once we'd find a way to come
through this dalliance of ours. Lightning strikes
the Empire State. Afterwards, hard rain speaks
volumes to empty streets in a language as fluid
as embraces throwing caution to the wind.
A force ten blows our hull and mast relationship
beyond Liberty. We will sail to the mouth
of the Bosphorus, where Judas trees bloom pink
over Istanbul in pursuit of Constantinople.

The Road to Butte

To Dermot McCabe

First I hears of Billing, Montana, is that television show, die-nasty, no Dynasty.
Later on Mum pipes up about some great-grand uncle of hers, William JJ Ryan
who married a well-to-do widow, letters say. From Billings Rimrock Trailways
I buys my return to Butte, gives it to Stanley, d'guy behind the Greyhound wheel.
A guy gets on with a see-through bag marked *patient belongings*, in indelible ink.
Two VETS trade Lucky Strikes for Nam tales…*can you imagine Altman's MASH
never spoke of us…Through early morning fog I see…nor…Visions of the things to be…*
Stanley helps bag-lady Ethel aboard, armed with her torn bin liner full of eighty
years and her bodies natural aroma without the benefit of a eau de toilet spray.
This might have been that Ranelagh lady, who wrote a remarkable short story,
though the city that never sleeps I think, is where she finally chose to stay.

Doors close, air comes on and we're off, leave Billings Rimrock to its Rim Rock.
The Rockies fill Stan's windscreen as if Sacré-Coeur, whitening chalk or snow on
d'Sugar Loaf before… *free Colombia Three*…catches your eye driving to Wicklow.
Low and behold…*A brave man once requested me to answer questions that are key…*
Metal bounces off tarmac as light off dark walls, walling weather from our Grey
-hound, drives through Main. Real touch of d'Wild West, a lot for Farm Machinery,
sells Ingian gear, feathered-stuff, the lot, no gates in sight, so we crosses the railway.
Two red-necks down the back in red-plaid shirts, brag about chicks they have had, all
the way from Grey Cliff till d'lady from Southampton thumbing Washington Square
tells them…*belt up, I've had more interesting fucks in trucks, Dodge pickups no
less…*opening up the foothills of the Great Plains leaves us aghast — breathless.

Heading west on Interstate 90, a city of freight trains block my pure clear vision
for miles, miles of black stuff cargo faces a dim grandiose trailer park community.
On route to Livingston a *Mountain Dew* billboard announces flea markets weekly
in permanent marker under *Thirst Quenched*, huge open spaces itself fill my view
bigger than the bus. On horseback with an iron will 'n hope in hand for a better life,
sees great-grand uncle Willy leave his Golden Vale with droves from Queenstown.
Weeks aboard a timber hull, cutting waves to the quick, to reach their promised land.
Where gold, silver and copper are like the wise men's gifts to a saviour, Amerigo'd
discovered. The Grand Canyon springs to mind, not to mention d'Virginia. Earth
mounds pimpled by ponderosa pines, others like little drumlins runs straight ahead.
Headlights beckon arrival of distance diminishing, as we pass by Pear Tree Ranch

a bit like Willy think'n Skellig Michael looms, closer he get's to Gustauv's Liberty.
Ellis names and numbers. Gold bugs weighs his head, so he heads towards the Rush
free from feudal system, the sweet dull promise of nothing and eking existence out.
Out of the horse's mouth it did come as clear as daylight, in a day to day sort of way
as an auld gravedigger would turn stiff clay, before worms aerate soil for rain to lay
its head upon, to burrow deeper, harder, into recesses of darkness, to find true black,
to know the other side of pitch is twenty-four caret fools gold and copper of earth's
black holes. For Berkley Pit, Alice Mine and d'giant Anaconda Mining Company
Marcus Daly from Ballyjamesduff recruits...Go West young man...posters all say.
Out d'window, it's all red-Indian country. At a pit-stop drive thru, smallest yet, seen
bigger garden sheds, sells: coffee and donuts, heavy ones with them chocolate rings on.

The Southampton doll's in search of a great-great someone 'n to see if ...suicide is
painless...as she roots for her Embassy mild red, ready for a Maguire and Patterson
flaring my palms, like fireflies reddening night's dark watch or the one her husband
shoots into d'navy sky, a shooting star marooned at sea, visible to the next generation.
Clings she does to that summer as if a plank of teak at sea, years float shipwrecked,
looking for dry land to place the first stake, indeed not that unlike young prospectors.
Great-great William Ryan of Lackabeg, whose mother came from far off Buffanoka,
one of granny Annie Ryan's brother's. With a gift of d'gab he happens upon many
a young widow at the Ancient Order of Hibernia's dress-ball, he'd throw d'odd eye
followed be d'greatest smelter in the world tour, before handing out Douglas Hyde
Cigars, flashed about as if King Edward's, the founder of our Land League was,

smoked be its members for a fee, in a pledge to help others. Take Charles Kennedy's
cork-foot, came from d'kitty so it did, later on he gets to own the Shamrock Saloon
where most hard rock punters are members, part gladly with their few bob for shots,
bars of Molly belted out...in Butte I stand no show...if jobs don't come, I'm on my
bum, Molly my Irish Molly O...'n for Godsake Don't go down the mines today, Dad...
So did great-great uncle Willy really resists Clan-na-Gael, Ribbonmen 'n Whiteboys
underground overtures? to raise hopes 'n funds for picnic-balls, to raise the gun and
d'glass, to toast good health and fortune, to brothers in arms, and to misadventures
of adventurers, all the whilst digging out Berkley Pit. Shallow breathing saves air,
with his shoulder to d'cart, jaundice light signals life and a canary's feathers flutter
as his Bella pushes the runt of their litter above ground, into their copper kingdom.

Its Lily O'Hara seen to them all, and them she's not, she minds as if prodigal son's and
let-on daughters, provides succour and sanctuary, is their pure saviour of souls.
Corduroy Road's red light district does a roaring trade. Caters for infidels 'n invalids,

43

heals like the touch of a saint or a rub of a relic, sells its wares to all God's children who may or may not be able to recite The Salve Regina, but in bits, *Hail, Holy Queen* comes with Acts of Contrition, adds commandments as Joe dreads the loss of heaven after daily mineshaft hell, he'd surly give young Dante's Inferno a run for its money were he to commit his day to paper or were he fluent in the Crown's tongue, foreign so it was like those bible ones that did talk of, what was it, some class of knowledge. As if portraits hung: handball alleys sport Gaelic job notices, *No English may apply to the Anaconda Mining Company.* Nature's call is answered in waste drifts, carbon

dioxide levels are tropical, depths of five-thousand coming up for air to minus forty. TB leaves Joe-Joe Casey with Galen Giggles at The Florence boarding house, fights for breath 'n shares lying down space, as fair weather miners escape *rocks on the chest. Don't Get Hurt, Ten Men Waiting For your Job.* In Hibernia Hall, young Willy drinks halfpints, hav'n passed hard rock grog-shops, orders drink till drunk, sees Jack Fogarty, from Keeper drown in rock blasts. His plan to buy a parcel of homeland sinks as if shafts or sloppy pints he skulls back. Jack's widow gets no dues, so Willy becomes *a fallen away Hibernian.* Four million tons of handmaid dynamite sticks blow up, extracts forty million copper tons. Single-jackers drive buzzies into dank depths, exploit auld codgers movements at *The Hospital* Number Two Shaft. At Cripple Creek they do holds-out for an eight hour day at three dollars fifty. Dare-devils burrow dust shafts as wild-cats strike.

Others die entombed like Egyptian Gods, in a sarcophagus of pure Protestant ore. In Finns, Italians, Croatian, and Austrian's the Irish loose their sure footing from, Joplin, Missouri, Spokane, Missoula they come to pick rock and ore, displace Dublin Gluch. As the Flathead reservation opens to white settlers, most have settled or cleared back to ranches and what with no Saloon to be opened on Indian territory, takers are few, unlike the day Father Jeremiah Callaghan does the warm up for our James Connolly. The place is mobbed, as if it might well be Sackville Street listening to The Liberator. Believe it or not, as America enters WW1 Dashiell Hammett works as a Pinkerton operative. Copper's demand has each mine flat out, what with every rifle shot, an ounce of pure Butte copper is lodged deep into layers 'n miles of young enemy flesh. Back on Interstate 90: hilltops jut out as if Cliffs of Moher with a sea of yellow-green

-tan below (no sea), dried and half-dried out lakes abound when the likes of Indians might charge down hillsides. On the hard shoulder, a dead deer sets the Southampton dolls off again...*the game of life is hard to play, I'm gonna lose it anyway, it brings so many...* Joining us at a pit-stop: an aboriginal with his didgeridoo and a shower of Mexicans the youngest one, fit as a fiddle, a scapular hangs from his neck, rubs his silver cross up that hits Maria's nose every Sunday morn as Ave is hymned out in Church as they reach

their own rhythm of breath, in tune with other bodies receiving holy sacraments.
God but they must have got bored, before billboards, signposts or tracks bisect openness,
before pylons, houses or tarmac carve roads through grasslands. Three Forks we
pass; pilgrimage to Our Lady of The Rockies. Inside we climb-climbs, reach a grotto.
Belief hangs from rafters, red round rosary beads, Kodak loved-ones lost to the earth,

thank-you's and dollar bills copper fastened to yew framed beams, does calls heaven
to indulge prayers inside Mary; Butte's own Liberty, sat upon The Continental Divide.
Fourteen Hall gallows frames dot Butte Hill, as if stations of d'cross after crucifixion.
Welcome to Butte, Silver Bow Country Heritage, drive past Copper Canyon Mansion
KFC 'n Taco Bell, our Greyhound does, station stops time's hem its very self, an after
life stillness exists in tall-pine shades as if Power Lalor's lodge in not far off Lackabeg
where Willy'd hand-catch salmon leaping up river, before Jimmy-gamekeeper catches
sight of darkness rustling. *For the Beara, Silvermines, Knockacappul 'n Matherclay
boys, say a Holy Mary,* Mammy Ryan's letters say, for them that daylights forgotten
who finds…*the game of life is hard to play*…no little house on d'prairie awaits, but dry
Foilduff soil under heavy arsenic-air, as if a pregnant raincloud waiting to give birth.

In the Village

On Canal Street you stumble into a quandary
of sorts, over the lateness of reclamation,
of the night you offered me the world on the flat
roof. Arms outstretched as if in veneration,
as possible futures rise amongst water towers,
against hammer and sickle, below cut and thrust
of Wall Street resting, yellow cabs hare through
Hemsley's arch as you arc me towards sky
scrapers, where the dark side of the moon
never seems brighter, constellations fall
into place, we trace bits of Orion and Little Bear
as though completing a jig-saw. Puzzle is, how
it all goes askew in sight of Bleecker and Tribeca.
Somewhere beyond Staten sirens are keening.

Feast of the Assumption

What of the day Ma sends Da for a half-dozen free-range, down
to Cavistons. Outside *Quinn's* (undertakers) he looses his return
with eggs in toe, as he has a half-kind of turn, turns out it's a black
-out. Not a shell breaks, nor orange-yoke splatters pavement cracks.
But hair-line cracks do appear, on a foreign consultant's X-Ray screen.
Exposes a geometry of interglacial action acting out of its own volition
again and again, repetitive movements seem to have shut down certain
parts, accentuated others to the point of no return like a circuit board
out of sync with itself. And unlike himself, he hears blue lines translated,
reads diagrams his body gives out, tells things he's not altogether ready
for. For he's not so far gone as to be lost in translation but has clarified
that his parts are wearing out like many d'Merc's he'd tinker with, always
at home under a bonnet, or finding the blown-white Christmas fairy
lights from Hector Grey's, strung out across the kitchen table as Ma'd
cut young turkey's neck with d'auld bread knife till her hands ran red.
She'd read the riot act to one and all, not to burst d'yellow gall bladder.
…*its all bladder if you ask me*…kidneys into the freezer for Bloomsday
and gizzards too… *tu-whit-awho*… you-who'd glue us to the spot alright.

So when Ma runs out of eggs again, off down the road he goes and goes still.
Wired that day so he was, like a suicide bomber, what with a square black
box strapped to his chest, his flight recorder of sorts, records he's out of sorts.
Eleven other black-boxes make their way from the outskirts to Heathrow.
Da, press green when your dizzy or light-headed, on the verge of a stroke.
By the time he finds his go button buried under his plaid red check shirt
and long-sleeved vest, they had been detected; he could have passed over.
Backpackers foiled in attempts; like those blasted fireworks blowing up d'sky
as the foghorn blows its horn for a new year, borne into damp dark, cartwheels
sunburst explosions are lost to rain, bells ring out heralding birth and renewal.
Sadam hangs. Look not away crowds capture mobile moments at breakneck
speed from Azerbaijan to Ballyjamesduff whilst Soldiers of Heaven crack on.

Feast of December Thirteenth

Into your field of vision, glazed over eyes like ones lost in veneration
or Saint Lucy's eyes offered on a plate; small cakes or biscuits eyeball
shaped, all ceremonies of light as if that brightness just before snow.

CUBA

To Martha Woodcock

Between your palms a mango imported beyond
Windward Passage softens, the heat of Yucatan Channel
knits towards ripeness, as ice cubes bruise mint leaves
in anticipating of Havana Club falling into company
with sugar cane. Mojito's like holy water come sundown
over Miramar prolongs its dying as though to play God.
Your Cadillac's fins sails under constellations
as if celestial trips for nomads. Climate change warns
of bigger storms at sea, of sirens in the wings,
and of colonial trade winds swaying ripe tobacco leaves.
And in the Waldorf Astoria, Romeo y Julieta
smoke wafts, small flurries of Pinar del Río's red earth
thickens circles as if fireflies caught in trees as fallen stars,
or is it more the little reliquaries of loss we construct.

Mass Rock at Glenstal

As I place my hands on the altar, a tingling slows
the contours of my fingertips, wells-up its topography
like an Ordnance Survey Sheet; number in relief,
or when ink from an immigration pad at Shannon left
a Hart's Tongue-print like the fern before me all over
this blessed flock wallpaper of ours; where I've traced
and retraced times spent listening to family histories,
the Rising, price of the pint and good weather for drying.

Teller

A green rubber thumb with hedgehog nipples
lifts note from note, counts the sum of currency.

In The Bank

Gertrude Lacy would sneak d'odd swig of her ball-o'malt, hid between
deposit and withdrawal slips. *Bank of Earland*, she would stamp on backs
of chicken's necks or *refer to drawer*, across their fronts with the effrontery
of CK2 emblazoned on chests. Bets she'd make with Terry Rogers, money
on at, Doncaster, Newmarket, The Curragh or Punchestown Two-Thirty's,
lucky dabbles, knobbed be a short head for falls at the first. As if night,
The Irish Field envelops her Calvita-moon-bread sandwiches, she swallows,
an equinox imprint of form, runners 'n riders and forecasts for d'Melbourne Cup.

Up on d'fifth, Les from Large Loans compromises Lucinda Knox from Stock
Issue, as Daff Wordsworth's double DD enters. Caught rapid they is, between
photocopier and fiche. Daff's Frapochino from Starbucks drops to ground
as Les lets Lucinda down...*God, can't find statements for d'tribunal enquiry*
Les says...*Daff, have you seen them?* Scarpers she does like an ostrich chick
in a flap, working out what, if anything she's seen at all. A ball-o'malt awaits
in her top desk drawer, bedded in bankers blank slips, she take a sip to her lips
as if pure holy water brought back from the Eucharistic Congress of Thirty Two.

Her head's a-go. Colour a-flutter in fact, as if the Papal Legate, Cardinal Lorenzo
Lauri's holy-show at Dún Laoghaire Harbour, kicks Congress Week's devotion off.
Papal Mass in Phoenix Park. Came from every corner they did (and again in Seventy
-Nine to see Karol Wojtyła) broadcasts from Rome, temporary shrines in tenements,
holy water fonts and rosary beads to beat the band, PA systems skywriting design of
the crowd, not so different to Nuremburg rallies our young Daff Wordsworth thinks,
as she runs her tongue-tip inside smooth pink fig skin, scoops seeds and swallows.
Allows ten minutes for a legget outside to Bessy's paper stand for *Woman's Way*.

Away with d'fairies she is. Hears John McCormack sing at High Mass, relayed by
BBC and Radio Athlone, (later Éireann), in Cosgrave 'n de Valera's yellow-white
papal days, bunting bears the brunt of ...*I can't see a blessed thing*... and ...*stop
waving blasted flags in me face*... or, *Daff,*... *have you got them MiWadi ice pops?*
Tops of the Town. Now there's a thing she'd not go in for. Too much familiarity,
hangers-on and over's, Daff thought. Though young Noreen Cooper in Chargebacks
is keen for it. Dressing up in daft rig-outs, cheeks dabbed with terracotta powder puff,
bears let-on heat of ancient Greece, her magnolia toga 'n crimson toes tempt Sunday

school black 'n whiteness of another age, challenges Rock of Ages 'n d'right of man…*for the kingdom and the glory*… Not even Marketing's Will Wood, would bother her. What with her de-glow highlighters, rainbow-arcs her oblong teak desk as Will lights Melinda Mary Duffy's dull days, cruciform across his pure oak desk, nests he does as if a chick after birth. Cert young Josh Washington from Projects is, of Jacinta Lucy's love for him, as she settles him, as if her Foreign Settlements or his olives 'n Feta fetish or of rice wrapped in spinach leaves, hunting green, giving it what for, all bluster and attitude she divvies his dividend portfolio up,

like the button-backed settee the Managing Director directs his latest conquest to. Sat upon his suede remnant from Murphy Sheedy, with the smell of new money folded in his palm, leaves ink in hand as if an aphrodisiac after the act. Pacts make money talk and gossip whisper like radio interference, static belts lights-out-of-day, to lessen Marjorie's haste, to kill her Call Centre pain like twists of lime Martini holds, coiled secrets fermenting gin and vodka, increases content beyond proof. Hoofs, Marjorie does, down passageways as if a Lacroix model down a catwalk, green rubber thumbs; pencil-crowned, 'n paper clips shudder their office earth.

Skirts Beth, John Jarvis does, 'n she that busy thumbing fifty's, quick as you like. Pike they eats d'night Zachariah Smith catches d'long arm of the law. Tying petty orange flies he was, after stuffing gullets with Charlie. High as gutted snow kites ground to a halt like faxes spewing figures out that don't add up, ended between desk-tops and slingbacks. Tacks, Ned Diplock thumbs to notice boards, get-to -gethers 'n d'rest like zest grated into Tom Collins' sat before upright Karaoke sub-committees night after blessed night, who fold their notes with a clean edge. Talk of files, configurations, spreadsheets, numbers spread across the haze of days

marks the Julian calendar. Click-clack, 'n tip-tap, tapping keys into words: bottom line, profit 'n loss, cutbacks and d'last of the wrapping paper, and the last of punch drunk fumbles in cubicles as Lucy Middleton is down on her knees. Investment protection she calls it, bank-ladder climbing, stumbles she does after turkey 'n ham over the MD's latest bit of up d'duff-fluff. Calls his bluff Lucy does, twists his arm, secures one hundred percent mortgage at low staff rates. Oh, but for the mediocrity of middle management, the price of free-range, ranging like line manager's meetings about meetings, its all rank and file, grades and gradation, shaves of a cult devotion.

Mrs. Arty Magoo

For the love of money, terrible things
Prudence did do, to rid herself of Arty

Magoo. You see she had such notions.
Not O'Casey's of avariciousness though

more, she deserved a place in the light.
In light of the fact that she'd won seven

long jumps and two or three cross country
hurdle thingamajigs, or such like yokes.

She has a verve for the edge of real things
imagined in unimaginable conditions,

favourable for sunny spells and scattered
showers, as a low lying depression fogs her

perspective of what passes before her eyes.
Buys time for her to process limbs at odd

angles, shadows wrestle darkness as moon
-light plays tricks, as if sequences on *Come*

Dancing, caught in the spin of a foxtrot sashay.
Says she'd swim the channel faster than a canoe,

knows her own mind, is what's mostly
said. Lead she was like an innocent abroad,

who'd lost her way down Venetian alleys
whose puddles wobble spires when stepped upon.

On account of her state of fairly graphic play
on Tiddley winks, and winking at young Ludo Lill,

chess was to find no home nor three card trick,
as Prudence turns d'odd trick, ménage à trois usually

la fresco, she has a weak spot for the bark of oaks
says it's the rough surface she's after, not the fall

of dappled sunlight clothing her body in after glow,
as glow worms come up for air as if stowaways.

Battle of Blue Licks

Always be sure you are right, then go ahead
—Daniel Boone

Murphy has the face of a man who over indulges, hankers after
old world species, some might say, for instance take Polly O,

from over the way. Always on hand, to lend a hand, or an ear.
Time was she'd lend a shoulder before Murphy unbalanced

her chip, now a blade is all she's good for. Having spayed
Murphy's pussy, he's not so precious anymore about fur.

Even his Davy Crockett hat made by real Greeks in Toronto,
from Russian skins, doesn't get the petting it once used to.

Though, hardly makes him King of the Wild Frontier, a back
woodsman, hunter or a trapper. More a Huguenot whose rifle

balls are wasted on a boy's missed shots. Coonskin cap in hand
and a bird in the bush leaves Murphy's hunger burrowing woody

wastelands, nuzzles damp wetness beyond the mouth of Nolichucky
river with a taste for rosehips. His whistles now, sing fluently as thrush.

Signalling Through Space Without Wires

I happened upon you in Lowestoft, no
less, of all places one might run into

an old flame, who'd managed to turn
me down-side-up, and outside-in.

Took me a good month of Sundays
it did to get over you. Its often not

great to dwell on such matters
that turns into worry beads, leads

it does to all kinds of stuff. Rough
class of dreams can deconstruct day

out of night and night out of day,
in pursuit of black holes and water

on Mars, never mind that broken
engagement you'd thought eternity

proof. In the pudding is where proof
hid, as you turn out hundreds a-pastry

lids, together with young Sid Lipton,
for cottage and Shepherd's pie crusts.

Lust they say drove you. Finds it hard
to imagine I does, even though the charge

sheet said, *cottaging in public lavatory*,
with a flock of George Michael look-alikes.

Fights broke out in the patisserie the likes
of which I'd not seen since Powell's Rivers

of Blood, back in sixty-eight. And Joan Rivers
providing alternative comedy down Broadway,

away from it all. Calls became far, far fewer
as if watching Marconi's dots and dashes cross

the ocean, then fade into rain. All that electricity
oscillating thoughts as radio waves lost at sea.

★ *Signalling Through Space Without Wires*, title of paper by William
Henry Preece (the Chief Electrical Engineer of the British Post
Office) introducing Marconi's ongoing work to the general public
at the Royal Institute on June 4th 1897.

Proof

From a Thwaite's Soda fountain you squirt a dash
of gas. Air breathes life into Gordon's and slice,

helps you cut to the chase, if not to put a finer
point on it. Between label's end and liquor

line, a clear light of day appears to be diminish
-ing percentage proof of sloes pure strength,

releases pent up thoughts shaping ideas in
to wordy words, escaping from your mouth.

By evensong, rows of empty stout bottles
hide as if fugitives under your stairs,

huddle dark warmth from extra strength
spilt porter, a brewery of sorts, a symmetry

of O's, craning their long brown glass necks
toward the light, as though waiting to be let out,

like off-license sales before closing time.
Time was, of a Christmas you'd get a delivery.

Come New Year, all ye faithful would go hand
to mouth for money back on Arthur's returnable's,

not to mention Mrs. Dew, who lives with a view
of the sea on her tablecloth. Some days, marmalade

perches high in the Amalfi coastline, on others, knobs
of butter appear to be Byzantium freezes coalescing

with light, makes a clear pathway through her love
of shapes, to her three sided Dimple Haig, an affair

conducted with the utmost passion for taste, stood
beside her Amaretto half moon's and extra virgin

olive oil. Her tabernacle of sorts, sorts thoughts
out, while she nibbles current-studded Garibaldi's,

runs her palms over labels with a reverence for holy
medals, like the ones she wears on her long-sleeved

swimming vest. Mrs. Dew dives for pink coral, baby
blue pearls and five starfish arms. Seldom she catches

more than sea shadows snorkeling her bathroom cork
floor, deep in recesses, sea lettuce, shingle 'n limbs lurk.

Beauty Spot

What springs to mind is a far off digging
sound, the likes of which you'd hear out
west, as if slabs of wetness are being cut,
as a sleán is driven through wild peonies, cotton
-grass, and flowering swathes of bull rushes.
Come dusk, turf pyramids scatter a dying
sun across lesser known layers, where bog oak
is sought after. It was our Cerberus drives home
the fact wee young Emily Rose Aldershot
had in fact been shot. Three bullets she took
to the heart his nose found, our curious little cocker
spaniel, not far below butterworth and sundew,
in her broderie anglaise holy communion frock.
Heather and blood-orange asphodels sway
as her white ribbon surrenders to inevitable dusk.

Flight Into

Whilst I hands you a baby
pyramid midstream,

of Toblerone, my fingers fall
into hieroglyphic grooves,

as if reading fossils I follows
Ra towards the eye of Horus'

thoughts, tip-toe through blue
dot-to-dot bottle tops; sand

constellations, ghost Carter
to the Valley of the Kings.

I intakes short breaths of dead
air in Tutankhamun's tomb,

come-to, to the scent of lotus
-lily fields in alabaster jars, adrift —

chariots, throne and papyrus
dice throwers move the afterlife

on, out of earth in to glass cabinets,
semi precious gold 'n ebony inlays

desire, makes a would-be thief
of your honest soul, fences black

markets galore sailing feluccas
up the Nile, pays your respects

between Luxor and Aswan
at Edfu, to the temple of Horus

as I breaks another pyramid off,
avenue of the sphinxes springs

to mind, leads on to the Karna
temple, whose myrrh trees yield

a gum that burns as incense
in our Pharaoh's sanctuary,

what with the rolling motion of
camels moving like ships

over oceans of sand in our
semi-detached little oasis.

Findings

There's a kind of a knack to this lark
of running the tip of your tongue

along the edge of darkness, fuses light
as if skinning-up. Up until now you

place worries one on top of the other,
building blocks for your Babel Tower

you says, babbling on about this or that
blaggard's figaries, chapels of ease and what

passes for please, greases palms as though
innuendo caught in the crevices of ideas,

sees trees bow to the print of a breeze
in far off images of its own window

reflection, happenings out of sight,
hedgerow holds garments strewn across

thorns of gorse, piercing the bias
of flaxen, yellowing the dying light.

Hemingway's Bathroom

Through half hoisted sash windows
at San Francisco de Paula, worn cords show.

The Spectator reads entrance hall light
travelling over empty bottles, well below

trophy heads hang, where family photos
might graft a natural chain of title over

attendants watch'n visitors not nick
trinkets for black market posterity.

The spine of *Houdini* tilts parallel
to a pickled lizard, who dared to kill

his cat, nearby a blue-green gazelle
shower curtain lies the frog that swam

with Ava Gardner, naked display
of ribbit, steeped in formaldehyde

captures her ephemeral beauty.
So, he'd touch its essence daily

for intoxication of sheer pleasure,
pure in the aftermath of its memory.

By a standee-up scales, walls record daily
weights, as if making notes for his novel:

stones, pounds, 'n ounces, graffiti-scrawls
reads with Wall Street Journal detail,

makes a strange algebraic motif of design
like a forgotten theorem awaiting proof.

His wooden garage houses mistresses
as if leaves raked in Fall, left to one

side for the fullness of time to decay.
Is it July's heat drives a gun

to his temple, amongst belly palms
'n hurricanes backing up weather systems?

By the Book

that's how they done
it, or let on at least.

Only that the train was dead
on time you could have spent

a night loitering by the kiosk
with a whole host of other dead

beats, beating time out of misery,
woebegone myths, and what if's,

as a Creole gardener waters birds
of his imaginary paradise by moon

light, illuminates a Caribbean heat
in each drop. Coconuts milk-heavy,

drops far beneath a palm canopy
as if spent bullets under the arms

of windmills, shelled in vain towards
a pale Cervantes shadowing forward

advances. Doctor's lance boils the size
of roses, making a fist of a blossom

bloom doubles inside delicate blueberry
cheeks as peaks 'n freaks asunder come,

all a, in cutting a dash mad sort-a-hurry,
like constant fear of a kind of purgatory,

or unmapped souls a-limbo left
weighing up what is right, or left

of wrong to balance right, as if a breeze
turning leaves into knowledge aforethought.

Fragrances

With a clear eye and a furrowed brow
as if veins of a heated rear window

melting frost, you acquiesce
with your petal-breath, of double

blossom roses, windblown,
tinged with a hint of weather

falling foul of Victorian pink
in battleship grey across parlour

walls, sentences ricochet as if bullets
punctuating talk from Tower Hill

and Foilduff to Castle Waller, Waller.

Rain on Longboat

To Chris and Ethna Lynch

There's a fog comes in for two
days, down from Atlanta, moves
southwards towards us,

as ships' long mast cuts clouds
to the quick, a beach boy bores
holes in sand, (erects umbrellas).

Pelicans skim ocean's breath
as if planes in-flight or a nib between
flow of ink to paper-touch where

angles of blackness joins sight
to sound meaning. Raindrops blot
as if a watercolourist's wash,

running reds down lifeguard
flags at lookout points, where manatee
are mistaken for white killers

and Joe Begley for Christ walking
on water, stood upon the arm of his catamaran,
hands cast out as if in prayer

sieving nets for fish, as his triangular
sail moves distance nearer and nearer
thy God to thee, before an applause

of rain plays hymns galore to ocean's floor,
joins swish to swash in a sepia mist
of what has passed and what is passing.

Whiteness

In Memory of Joan O'Hara

What with the swimming motion of fish
you sees order redefine the scheme of things.

The Cassini Gap of Jupiter's moons,
Newton's inverse square law of gravity pulls

your thinking in unimagined directions;
towards the behaviour of oscillating systems,

astronomical works touching the Spring
of Air, as the splish-splash of rain globes

dropping as if nails driven into palms,
creates handfuls of doubting Thomas's,

fluid 'n as changeable as weather itself
leaves no certainty but for imagined charts

forecast tales of other perceptible likelihoods
either long or short range. Strange how it seems

roundness disperses itself in uneven arcs: moons,
pupils and belly buttons galore, does light sight

-chords' underbelly, indolent mandolins
pregnant with tunes melodious to the deafest ear

spills — hears concertos you does, sees architecture
of trees suspend an orchestration of snowflakes,

turrets and draw bridges melt into castle moats,
floats into the nothingness that is everything.

Gone are the Lightships

Though folded away in the lining of a pocket
you arrive unannounced as if a change

in weather, alter the climate of my thoughts
like a gulf stream's warm air,

a breath of ease insects can ride
to fathom the calculus of flight.

And when I lay down the words
like an offering of sorts,

you expose whiteness,
keeping desire at bay.

From deep inside it comes, like a longing
to drive across the Golden Gate

uninterrupted by the thought of you unravelling
the storm we gather and weather
in the face of what we have disfigured of ourselves.

ANNE FITZGERALD is a graduate of Trinity College, Dublin and Queen's University, Belfast. Her collections are *Swimming Lessons* (2001) and *The Map of Everything* (2006). She is a recipient of the Ireland Fund of Monaco Literary Bursary at The Princess Grace Irish Library in Monaco (2007). She teaches Creative Writing in Ireland and in North America. She lives in Dún Laoghaire, Co. Dublin. For further information see www.fortyfootpress.com